Scarlet fades

Aireanna Anderson

Scarlet fades © 2022 Aireanna Anderson

All rights reserved.

Presentation by *BookLeaf Publishing*

Web: www.bookleafpub.com

E-mail: info@bookleafpub.com

ISBN: 9789357618021

First edition 2022

For my mom, for always pushing me and
helping me through my emotions,

I love you

Poisoned Mind

How can I patch up my broken mind again
With false happy memories
And an overused thread

How can I take back my thoughts of suicide
In these glass goodbyes
The shards shatter and spread
And wound the ones I love

They leave splinters in the hearts of those I'll
leave behind
How can I burden them with my life
But how can I burden them with my death
How can I patch up my broken mind again

These episodes are long and draining
But I'm seasoned in this pain
Like the elite warriors of an ancient land
I fight to survive
I fight to make a change

To transform my mind into something tangible
Something I can feel
Something I can mold into anything but what it
is

For I'm so exhausted by my thoughts
My mind
The screams
The voices never stop
They just change speeds

Like an overstimulated enemy
It charges in without a plan
Yet dismembers my already breaking body
With its shaking bloody hands

Yet it wants me to use the blade
To cut out my own heart
To stop my breathing
To make me depart

My mind is in turmoil
It's always at war
I'm stuck in this never ending terror

I'm fighting to hold myself back from the ledge
To stop from falling from this cliff of regrets
I'm fighting not to listen to the sounds
In this mind so loud
I'm screaming out

Can I patch up my mind
Is it too late to see

I don't really want to die
I just want to stop the pain
To make it leave

It's like a poison inside
Infecting all I do
I finally stopped this mind of mine
Now that my heart has stopped too

Background Noise

The thoughts in my head
Are louder than you know
Like background noise
At a concert
And my death will be the show

The screams that I hide
Are distant
Because I don't want you to see
That even though I have your love
My scars still run deep

I'm trying not to listen
As the thoughts parade my mind
But deep inside the demons creep
Whispering "leave this all behind"

I'm slowly losing ground
As this war still rages on
The demons and the voices both
Tell me that I'm wrong

My strength is depleting
I can't fight this on my own
But deep inside, locked away

There's a darkness I don't know

And if I lose one more battle
That darkness might overflow
And finally consume
What's left of me
I can't win if I'm my own enemy

Demons at the Door

Do I listen to myself
Or the demons at the door
I can't find some peace of mind
All these thoughts begging for more

Do I listen to my heart
Or my overtaken mind
These demons and the voices
Telling me to leave it all behind

For It all breaks inside
like the ashes of you and I
It all pours like rain
Through the neverending showers of pain

That I feel so intensely
It stops my breathing for a while
I can't move
It's deadly

These thoughts that beg for more time
They just want to stay alive
They just want to be heard
But they aren't me
They are the reflection of myself

The one that wants to get help
The one that's buried deep inside
The one that will be sacrificed

For I let the demons in
They were pounding on the door
Now I'm locked away
Begging to be heard
Like the voices were before

Down

I was younger than I thought
When I first tried to die
I was younger than I wanted
When I first grabbed a knife

I took too many pills
I couldn't even cry
Yet here I am, still standing
But where do I reside

I'm here but my mind is shaken
It struggles to survive
When everything inside is breaking
When I can't see the light

But in this darkness, I feel comfort
For it is now my home
And in this darkness, I feel closure
For I finally know where to go

Down
Down I go
Until my lungs can't breath

Down

Down I go
Until my hands can't claw the dirt anymore

I know that I can't win
But if I find a way to hide
Then maybe I can stay
Maybe then I'll want to find a way

Crossfire

Caught in the crossfire
Thought I was safe
From all of the memories
That hold in my rage

Caught in the crossfire
There's no escape
I can't remember
All the glimpses of pain

But my body feels it
The hands on my neck
I don't remember
But my body reacts

I'm held captive
My hands are in chains
As my mind wanders through
This blood filled maze

I try not to look
But my eyes are glued
To the fading images
Like they're not something I lived

But something I saw
Like a tv screen in a cinema

There's a shooter here
Inside my brain
These bullets destroy
All that remains

For how can I move on If I cannot see
All that is broken
All that's happened to me

All I want is to forget but I can't regret this
For I wasn't at fault
I was too young to know to scream
I was too young to know anything
I was too young to not believe

Purple Sky

Slowly now
Don't break the fall
It's over now
We lost it all

Slowly now
Take my hand
I'll lead you to a stranger land

Where the sky is a deep dark purple
And the world, it glows

Where there's a moon for the moon
And there's always snow

Slowly we will go
Surely we will fall
Away from all the eyes
That watched and judged us all

Where the trees grow higher than the birds can
fly
Where you want to live and you don't want to
die

I'll take you to this strange new place
In our minds
In this haze

Just know that you are not alone
I'll carry you until it feels like home

Until your eyes fade from view
I'll hold you until you lose this too

Slowly now
Don't break the fall
For in the morning
The sirens call

Slowly now
We lost it all
I held your hand
Till it lost its grip
You were always the best of this

A Strangers hand

I'm standing on a ledge
It's about to break
I don't know where I am
Or just what's at stake

My heart's about to bust
From all my grave mistakes
I don't want to fall
But I can't live this way

There are voices in my head
They don't sound like my voice
They're telling me to jump
Like I don't have a choice

I'm afraid of heights
Yet I can't want to look away
For if I take a step
Maybe then I'll find a place

A place for my soul to finally get some sleep
A place for my heart to rest
A place I can keep going on
Without so much pain
A place I can feel at home

Without giving myself away

But this ledge won't hold for much longer
I'm losing hope that I'll find anything at all
Inside this dreadful life
But if I keep on going
Maybe I can survive

I'm standing near a ledge
It collapsed in front of me
A stranger's hands hold my waist
I didn't fall
Neither did they
We both got up
We walked away

Crashing

It comes in waves
So willing to escape
But the fire won't behave
Deep inside me

When everything is great
There's no reason to break down
But once the crash rolls in
I'll surely drown

I'll start to shake
From everything I'm feeling
My mind is a place
I don't want to be hiding from
Yet here it comes again
A wave of mixed emotions

Is my afterglow
Too dim to be seen
Is my inner glow
Something far beneath

Am I too late now
To stop this rollercoaster I'm on

For its about to crash down to the ground
Cause I can't feel right now

I don't know what's worse
Feeling nothing or it all
But deep inside
Down below
I'm so lost I can't even fall anymore
Into the abyss of my mind
I can't find the light
I can't close my eyes

I can't find the time
To be something great
If all I do
Is judge my mistakes

These crashing waves
Are killing me
These ups and downs
Are like a bad dream
That plays on repeat

These screams I cry
can't be heard
If I let go
Would this still hurt

I don't know what's worse

Living or dying
But right now I'm trying to find a way
Do I have the strength to stay

Holding myself

What the hell am I doing
Looking into the mirror
Staring down at my reflection
Am I really here

What the hell can I even say
I'm so scared to tell you no
But how can I stay this way
Is there shame in letting go

How can I keep doing this
If I can't love you right
How can I try to mend this
Should I finally say goodbye

Why the hell am I not good enough
Why am I still standing here
On the ground
I rest my head
Because you don't want me near

I'm so sick of saying It'll all be fine
So sick of trying not to fight
Is there shame in letting go this time

Is there shame in letting go
I'm on the ledge
I need to know

Just how deep do you want to go
Your hands are blades
And they know
Just where to hold me
To cut my body from within

Now even my reflection is bleeding
Am I ready to give in
But what the hell are you doing
If you love me why do you hurt me
Every change you get

So is there shame in letting go
I'm crying out
I need to know

For your love is something
I thought would hold me
Not break me
Not cut me or shape me
Into something I don't recognize

Now I'm letting go
It is time
For me to hold myself up

And heal the wounds
You scared me with
But I'll be okay
Because I can say
I'm the one that got away

Keeping me

Sleeping
All alone I can't see if you're taking with me
I don't know where to go
I'm leaving my mind
and this world behind

Lying
I can't tell just how much I'm lying to you
I don't know what to do
I can't seem to open up
I don't think I'm good enough for you

For I can cut but I don't feel
I run away
When it feels real
I'll fight but don't know why
I feel such judgment in their eyes
In your eyes

Weeping
In my body, I hear weeping
I don't know if it's my heart
Or my head that I'm killing
But it hurts my soul

Take away this pain
I want to fly away
I want to soar beyond the clouds
Where my mind can find solitude
From all the sounds and the screams
From these hallucinations that I see

Keeping
I can feel myself keeping everything inside
So many reasons to hide, from even myself
Can anybody help
Can anybody see
I'm fighting just to show myself the real me

Still Fighting

I held onto my mind
A constant reminder
That I am not okay
I held onto my heart
Before I let it slip away

From the thoughts that waged so many wars
It's a battle every day
And it's exhausting
I'm in a war zone
Killing time
As the demons try to fight my every move

I am so tired
I can't even breathe at night
All I want is to stop this fighting
But if I stop for just a moment
I'll lose the battle you so desperately want me to
win
But I just want to feel again

You know I'm not okay
You see the demons that I face
But you don't know how strong they have
become

They've sharpened their blades far more than
once

You know I've beaten the odds
So why can't I let go now
I lived past what everyone thought I could
Now I just seek the home I've never seen
A place with no misery

I've felt it once before
As a child yet it was fleeting even then
I barely remember a time when
I wasn't at war with myself
Fuck this mental health
I can't seem to shake

The mania keeps me going
When I want to end the pain
The depression is a dagger
A poison tipped bloody blade
The voices keep on yelling
They never want to sleep
The visions shake and scare
Even the worst in me

But I'm still fighting
I'm still here
I just want a moment
To let go of this fear

That the pain will never end
As the war still rages on
I've become stronger than I was
But the demons haven't ceased
I'm fighting every day
But I'm angry

Why should I have to live this way
Why should I have to fight to stay
Why can't I hold my mind like it wasn't trying to
hurt me
I'm losing from the bruisings it inflicts
I can't fight this
I can't win
I can barely even stand anymore

I'm so tired
I crave to sleep
To stop this painful melody
To find some inner peace
To end the war inside me

Attack

Punch
Another hit as I try to move
I tried to forget all I've been going through

Break
Something is breaking inside of me
I've taken so many beatings

I crave the darkness to invoke another life
Surrounded by a forest of memories
I could never be what I want

For I'm chasing after a ghost
An illusion
A fragment of my past
One I could never be again

Happy
That's what I used to feel
Something I long for but can't seem to find
Something has died inside me

My mind's a hierarchy
It's the ruler of my soul
My mind is in chaos

For I was lost long ago

These ancient ruins that I now call home
Is full of snake that's venom will paralyze
And I've been bitten too many times

This progress I've made
Seems to only be an inch
In the mists of a galaxy that's far and reaching
As gravity holds me down to earth

Yet I'm fading fast
I'm not meant for this

Punch
Another hit as I try to move
I've only defended myself from the attack
To win I'll have to learn to punch back
To win I'll have to learn to live again

Hope

Lost in this moment
Trying to hold in
All these emotions
That want me to end this

Locked in a daydream
Where no one can hurt me
But all of these feelings
Are suffocating me slowly

I want to say I'm fine
But I know that's a lie
I don't want to show you
This madness
But you could save my life

So I'll tell you my truth
I don't want to fight this battle anymore
Please won't you let me shut this door
That let the demons in
I don't want to win

I just want to let it go
Let my grip let loose
I just want to find a new path

I don't want to lose myself this way

It's cutting into my soul
I'm tired of living and breaking down
But I won't lose hope
That my days will find a way
To break open and show the light that I once
knew
Instead of this fog that haunts me

I plead with myself to finally let go
Of all the hate inside
This meaningless genocide of myself
It's breaking and I'm helpless against it
Why can't I let go of it all
why can't I see that I'm still standing

So I'll tell you my truth
I don't want to fight this anymore
but I won't let it win
there's still hope
I can defeat them

Forehead Kisses

Your forehead was a place for kisses
Your eyes, a gate to your soul
I'll miss you when you were singing
From "knock three times" to rock and roll

You were a voice of reason
You were always one to stay
I wished you'd live forever
Who knew there would come a day

A day of no more forehead kisses
A day with no more light
For you took it all when you went away
Took my love and my might

Now, standing in the dark
I hear footsteps all around
Hoping desperately that there are yours
but they never will be again
For you have met your end

But your love is here to stay
Behind my forehead where your kiss would be
I'll hold onto this memory
I know you're still here with me

Unite

This place is swarming with monsters
Even now I can hear their cries
But it's not the demons I'm afraid of
It's the fading in your eyes

Your hand held my heart
Until your grip began to leave
You were always my direction
Now in this moment, I'm lost at sea
I can't believe this is happening

I touch your skin as your life fades out
I close your eyes with a tear
I feel like my soul is broken
We could have had so many years

The screams are getting louder
As the hoard still fights to kill
But I'm sprawled out on the floor
For next to you is where my blood will spill

As my lifeless body lays against yours
I don't regret a thing
Now I know even after death
Our stars shine deep in the sky

We are one, as we unite
We never have to say goodbye
We never need to close our eyes
We'll be together till the morning's rise

Oil and Water

This false illusion
A trick of the soul
A swarm of memories
Convince us both

These knives cut through
All that's real
Like a constant presence
To numb the truth

Of what we're feeling
In a moments heart
We are not broken
But we were torn apart

A pulse of feelings
Left us without control
A moments weakness
Turned us into a ghost

We were like oil and water
A vibrant atmosphere
But when the heat came over
We blow and disappeared

I could not escape
Our love was an overdose
I tried to push through
But I hurt us both

Now my waters frozen
Everything's so cold
This dark illusion
Left me too hard to hold

Now I'm a life untold
Yet forward I will go
Unto the dark unknown

Merry-go-round

I keep crying but I don't know why
Too many tears will drown my eyes

I keep falling through the steps I take
Stuck in a well now
I can't escape

I'm afraid of these feelings
That won't stop pouring like rain
But I'm afraid of the emptiness
This drought of mistakes

I can't recognize what I can do to replace
All this anger and pain
That keeps counting my days

I'm so sick of this fight
But I can't lose
I'm so sick of this life
I don't know what to choose

It's like a merry-go-round
And It can't be stopped
Because there are monsters that lurk
Monsters that block my line of sight

I can't run away
They follow and they watch
Every step that I make

I'm not trying to confine myself to this ride
But I'm stuck and I'm scared
I just want it to end
But I can't change the speed
For I'm not in control
This life's the one that's controlling me
This merry-go-round will be the death of me

Bloom

Self destructive
My mind is numbing
My heart won't beat
I'm unbecoming

Self isolated
In my own world
I'm completely unstable
Don't want to move a muscle

For it burns inside
With these demons I hide
With all my pain
I cry myself to sleep

When I'm all alone
I still hear screaming in my mind
When I want to live
I still want to die

I'm a walking suicide
A ticking bomb
Telling a time it won't remember
Yelling inside a quiet room

I'm falling from a nightmare
Where I seem to always bloom
Cause inside this dark depression
That is where I feel at home

Inside this dreary melody
Of the chaos I consume
This is where I'm meant to be
Inside this numbness that makes me
Self destructive and deadly
I'm alone but not lonely anymore

White Walls

These four white walls
Padded with pain
Protect me from myself
Until my blood rains down

These hospital gowns
Don't fit me right
I'm lost inside a broken mind
A constant fight from suicidal rage

I don't want to play this game of pretend
Where I hold my head up and say I'm fine
Where I close my eyes and open them again

I don't want to open them again
I want to sleep
I'm tired

But not the kind of tired I can wake up from
Not the kind of tired I can dream away
Not the kind of tired I can sleep off

I'm tired of myself
My mind
My thoughts

The screams that haunt me
The blood that doesn't drip deep enough

I'm just so tired
And I just want peace
Why couldn't I find a way
To be normal
To not feel so strange
Every waking day
Every hour passed

I just want to hold on
But I'm losing grip on reality
My mental health is killing me
Will it be the death of me

Will I be just another statistic
Or will I beat the odds
And one day become stronger than I am
Will I become whole again

Except I haven't been whole since I was a child
Running for miles from a nightmare I can't
escape
For I saw all these monsters that no one else
could see
I saw the faces of demons when I went to sleep

Hoping they would take me away

And I wouldn't wake up
Hoping they were nicer than the people
That hurt me
Because how could they be worse
Even with their horns and broken smiles
They looked at me
Not through me

Hoping these monsters would consume me
Until I wasn't real
Until I didn't have to feel
Everything and nothing all at once

This heaviness is like a loaded gun
Pointed at my head
But I can't pull the trigger yet
For I'm paralyzed even from death
I'm frozen in the pain
These four white walls
Drove me insane

Shadows Grip

Into the darkness, they roam free
Wearing masks and crowns of thorns
Claws as sharp as a dagger's blade
Heads matched with bloodied horns

They stalk and watch me patiently
Waiting for a chance
To rip apart the best in me
Always waiting for a glance in their direction
For these demons that I see
Reside in shadows in my mind
And shadows on the ground
As they linger all too close
To this life that I have found

Their claws have touched my skin
A map of scars in their place
I'm covered by terror when I see a shadows face

My body is a punching bag
For these rouge nightmares
I don't know if I can escape their grip
When I'm lost in this darkness

For at first they were so kind

Now I'm trapped here in their cage
Made of thorns and spikes and spines
But I can't see beyond this haze

And as I lay in this chamber of fear
I see nothing but my broken mind
That was so vibrant once before
But at last, the darkness roared
And took away my sight
Run while you still have time

For If you see a shadows face
Pretend you see right through
For If you look away too soon
They will come and they won't wait
Their claws will catch you
You can't escape

Scarlet fades

Scarlet fades into the night
As my blood drips
From these wrists of mine

Scarlets fades
I closed my eyes
It's too late now
I've said goodbye

Scarlet rises
In the morning sky
A sun so radiant
It glows all night

Scarlet fades
The moon must shine
As I slip into an endless silence

Say you loved me
I know that's true
But my Scarlet bleed
From me to you

Say you miss me
I hope you'll live on

I just couldn't fight
I couldn't overcome

All the stitches I tore
All the blood I bleed
I tried to live
But I couldn't pretend
I was okay any longer
I finally shut this door

Scarlet fades
One last time
As I look and watch
The clear moonlight

Scarlet fades
I closed my eyes
One last time
I'll say goodbye

Printed in the USA
CPSIA information can be obtained
at www.ICGtesting.com
LVHW021551211223
766988LV00097B/5683